WHITHER CAMBODIA?
Beyond the Election

The **Institute of Southeast Asian Studies (ISEAS)** was established as an autonomous organization in 1968. It is a regional research centre for scholars and other specialists concerned with modern Southeast Asia, particularly the many-faceted problems of stability and security, economic development, and political and social change.

The Institute is governed by a twenty-two-member Board of Trustees comprising nominees from the Singapore Government, the National University of Singapore, the various Chambers of Commerce, and professional and civic organizations. A ten-man Executive Committee oversees day-to-day operations; it is chaired by the Director, the Institute's chief academic and administrative officer.

The **Indochina Unit (IU)** of the Institute was formed in late 1991 to meet the increasing need for information and scholastic assessment on the fast-changing situation in Indochina in general and in Vietnam in particular. Research in the Unit is development-based, with a focus on contemporary issues of political economy. This is done by resident and visiting fellows of various nationalities, and to understand the Vietnamese perspective better, the Unit also has a regular programme whereby scholars from Vietnam are invited to do research on issues of topical interest.

WHITHER CAMBODIA?
Beyond the Election

Timothy Carney
Tan Lian Choo

Indochina Unit
INSTITUTE OF SOUTHEAST ASIAN STUDIES

*Cover photo by Jonathan Drake
shows an UNTAC official
updating an election tally board
in Phnom Penh, 1993*

Published by
Institute of Southeast Asian Studies
Heng Mui Keng Terrace
Pasir Panjang Road
Singapore 0511

All rights reserved. No part of this publication may be reproduced, stored in a retrieval system, or transmitted in any form or by any means, electronic, mechanical, photocopying, recording or otherwise, without the prior permission of the Institute of Southeast Asian Studies.

© 1993 Institute of Southeast Asian Studies

Cataloguing in Publication Data

Carney, Timothy.
  Whither Cambodia? : beyond the election / Timothy Carney and Tan Lian Choo.
  1. Cambodia–Politics and government–1975-
  2. Elections–Cambodia.
  I. Tan, Lian Choo.
  II. Title.
DS554.8 C28   1993   sls93-75459

ISBN 981-3016-62-0
ISSN 0218-608X

The responsibility for facts and opinions expressed in this publication rests exclusively with the authors and their interpretations do not necessarily reflect the views or the policy of the Institute or its supporters.

Typeset by International Typesetters
Printed in Singapore by Scapa Pte. Ltd.

*Dedicated to the memory of
Professor K.S. Sandhu
Director of ISEAS, 1972–1992*

CONTENTS

Compromise and Confrontation: The Cambodian Future
　Timothy Carney　　1

The Cambodian Election: Whither the Future?
　Tan Lian Choo　　18

Discussion　　29

About the Authors　　52

COMPROMISE AND CONFRONTATION
The Cambodian Future

Timothy Carney

INTRODUCTION

The international community as a whole and ASEAN in particular have paid in diplomatic and political capital, in dollars and in blood to effect a solution to the Cambodia problem that works. Singapore led a successful diplomatic pressure campaign throughout the decade after Vietnamese forces chased the Democratic Kampuchea regime from Phnom Penh. In the United Nations Transitional Authority in Cambodia (UNTAC), Singapore's police have been effective as have Singapore civilians, including one who served as the Information/Education Division Chief of Production with the vital role in assuring Cambodians their vote would be secret. The Indonesian venue for the Jakarta Informal Process and role as Co-Chairman of the Paris Conference concluded with the dispatch of Indonesian troops as part of the peacekeeping battalions. Malaysian police and military worked effectively under UNTAC's mandate. Philippine police formed part of the UNTAC effort. Thailand's role as staging point, provision of UNTAC military engineering support and key role as the frontline state in diplomacy need no elaboration.

The Paris mandate changed. The refusal of the Party of Democratic Kampuchea (PDK) to canton its troops and disarm and to give UNTAC access to its zone made the comprehensive political settlement to the Cambodia conflict envisaged in the 23 October 1991 Paris Agreement impossible to effect. Instead, an adapted mandate aimed to create a new Cambodian government with domestic and international legitimacy. The May election evidenced a massive popular will for peace. By early July, the Constituent Assembly Standing Committee on the Constitution had begun daily meetings, divided into small groups to discuss the vital elements of a Constitution such as separation of powers. The process of political compromise has begun with the creation of a Provisional National Government to assure the interim until the new constitution appears.

The complex and painful process has forged new possibilities for the U.N. role in the modern era, defined its limits and tested the world community. The vigorous debate over the larger implications promises lively discussion, multiple dissertations, and work for institutions and think-tanks well into the future.

This present discussion deals primarily with the internal, the Cambodian dimensions without, however, slighting the reality of external influences.

BACKGROUND

The past weighs as heavily on Cambodia's future as any historian could possibly conceive. The glories of the Angkor civilization contrast in the starkest imaginable terms with the chaos and the moral and political bankruptcy of the recent past. This situation is exacerbated, if it is possible for it to be worsened, by the persistent Cambodian suspicion of their Vietnamese neighbours' intentions. This suspicion, based in the reality of territorial losses and cultural imperialism of the nineteenth and twentieth centuries, has now become a devastatingly self-defeating obsession within the traumatized Cambodian body politic.

The tragedies of the more than forty years since Norodom Sihanouk's coronation engender the fear among some foreign and many Cambodian intellectuals and analysts that political maturity may never develop. This is despite the sophistication the electorate showed making their political choices in May 1993. Poor political institutionalization and limited opportunity for a civil society to develop remain key to the medium- and long-term future of Cambodia.

Fortunately, the discredited and largely discarded ideology of Marxism-Leninism remains in Cambodia only in the leading elements of the increasingly marginal Communist Party of Kampuchea (the Pol Pot–led "Khmer Rouge").

Ideology is less of an issue among the leading Cambodian politicians of the largest political factions. The issues centre on interest and the possibility for altering coalitions are real. Unfortunately, only rarely is the national interest credited as of supreme importance.

POLITICKING AND POLITICS

Factional interests before the election centred on very different analyses of their prospects. Smaller parties, that is, those other than the "big four" of the Cambodian People's Party (CPP), FUNCINPEC, the Buddhist Liberal Democratic Party (BLDP) of Son Sann and its fellow offshoot from Son Sann's Khmer People's National Liberation Front (KPNLF), the Liberal Democratic Party (LPD) of Sak Sutsakhan, hoped for enough seats to become coalition brokers. Results deceived them all.

The electorate clearly preferred the two largest parties, CPP and FUNCINPEC. Even the LDP, which had hoped, as one of its active candidates optimistically told me, for up to twenty seats, got none. The BLDP, which led an active, credible campaign, received only ten seats. This disappointing result occurred, despite the opening of numerous party offices and an active campaign of rallies. When taken with the poor showing of other parties, it reinforces the view that the popular will centred on the CPP or FUNCINPEC.

The CPP

CPP electoral efforts divided into an open campaign and a clandestine effort at intimidation. The open effort appealed to the rational and to the emotional experiences of the electorate. The incumbent, for that is what the CPP effectively was, used the ubiquitous campaign presence of one of Cambodia's most palpably effective politicians, Hun Sen, to remind the voters that the CPP was the only bulwark against the hated Khmer Rouge; and that FUNCINPEC was an old and probable future ally of the genocidal red Khmer. The extent of reliance on Hun Sen can be seen in speeches of CPP Chairman Chea Sim, who included regular reference to Hun Sen's own speechmaking.[1]

The CPP abused its dominating relationship with the State of Cambodia (SOC) to claim far more air time for CPP activities than UNTAC regulations permitted.[2] The Chea Sim remarks above, for example, were broadcast during reports of dedications of new schools, a non-campaign activity. This transparent device violated electoral campaign regulations.

A clandestine CPP effort to undermine its electoral opposition began in 1992. It included both violence and the use of secret police groups to identify "targets" and to engage in dirty tricks, including fomenting louts to harass opposition parties. Propaganda served to legitimize these covert activities. The legitimate opposition was described pejoratively and their activities equated to the worst crimes. Members of the opposition were limned as either criminal or Khmer Rouge elements. Members of the SOC and CPP seemed to take such exaggerated or fanciful charges seriously. Bangkok-based journalist Jacques Bekaert described an SOC police group identified as "A92", citing a confidential memo of the Ministry of National Security as indicating a plan to "win the trust of the opposition parties so as to create the conditions for seizing control of their most important functions" and to "carry out ... the destruction and forestalment of the ... activities of the opposition parties".[3] Bekaert notes that he does not know if the activities were ever carried out.

The SOC-sponsored campaign of violence, including murder, against opposition parties that began in September of 1992 reached a high point in December as opposition parties increasingly located offices in the provinces. The campaign continued into 1993 and UNTAC's Human Rights component listed fifty incidents of harassment, or of violence including murder, in the period 1 March to 14 May 1993.[4] Convincing evidence that the campaign had central backing was failure by the authorities to prosecute any of the perpetrators, as the Special Representative of the Secretary General (SRSG) had called for in his statement to the Supreme National Council (SNC) of 10 April 1993.[5]

By the end of the campaign period, however, and despite public statements about taking 70 per cent of the vote, leading CPP figures were said to be worried.

FUNCINPEC

Meanwhile, Prince Norodom Ranariddh's movement had shed the euphoria of popular embrace it enjoyed in the heady days of late 1992. FUNCINPEC leaders feared that SOC/CPP intimidation, combined with the reality of Democratic Kampuchea fighting had put the party's electoral chances at question. Prince Ranariddh and his senior staff increasingly leaned on the Vietnamese issue, tarring the CPP with the Hanoi brush as vigorously as the CPP used the myth of FUNCINPEC under the covert Khmer Rouge control against the royalist party.

FUNCINPEC media crossed the line to incitement to racial hatred in an effort to woo voters, traditionally suspicious of Vietnamese activities and intentions towards Cambodia. A cartoon in the Party youth magazine viciously recalled one of the popular memories of the nineteenth century when Vietnamese forces would bury three Cambodians up to their necks, light a fire to boil water for tea, and urge the victims not to shake the kettle. UNTAC Information/Education Division required a senior FUNCINPEC official to re-record a video political statement that risked incitement in its language excesses referring to the CPP debt to the Vietnamese. (He then complained to the press about UNTAC censorship.)

In the end, however, FUNCINPEC's line of negotiation and reconciliation seemed to touch the popular will to see peace. Prince

Ranariddh had particularly stressed this position at what became a FUNCINPEC Congress in February at Rumchong in their zone. He said that a winning FUNCINPEC would need all the civil servants, police, and military to make Cambodia run.

As the election approached, leading FUNCINPEC figures were unsure of the extent of their vote. Prince Ranariddh was said to maintain a "victory" was at hand and to do so in the face of scepticism even from his father. But other FUNCINPEC figures would not even predict an electoral plurality.

AFTERMATH

The election produced two large fragments. FUNCINPEC took a plurality of 45 per cent, which translated, under the proportional system by province, to fifty-eight seats. The CPP took 38 per cent, or fifty-one seats. Son Sann's BLDP gained ten seats and the millenarian Moulinaka Party, whose leader received UNTAC's ultimate sanction of removal from candidacy for violations of the electoral law, got one seat.

The nature of Cambodia's political experience caused the CPP to react badly to failure to win a majority. CPP leaders first tried to silence Radio UNTAC's broadcasting of partial results beginning on 29 May. They protested dissemination of news that indicated they were not winning, even though the SRSG had informed the Supreme National Council that morning that UNTAC would announce results twice daily. CPP leaders then adopted the device of citing a number of irregularities such as broken ballot box seals, in a transparent attempt to put the results of the election at question.

Meanwhile, intensive politicking began. One, or perhaps two, Cambodian People's Armed Forces (CPAF) Generals sought to see

Prince Sihanouk. They saw Princess Monique instead. On 1 June Chea Sim met with Sihanouk and requested the Prince to arrange a meeting with Prince Ranariddh to effect a national reconciliation and realize the popular will for peace. Prince Ranariddh, who had left Phnom Penh after the vote, almost certainly for reasons of personal security, did not reply to initial palace invitations to such a meeting. On 2 June Prince Sihanouk wrote to his son about a meeting, but received no reply.

On 3 June Hun Sen and Chea Sim met with the Prince, asking him to assume all power. Phnom Penh circles mooted possible violent activity against UNTAC and/or FUNCINPEC by SOC Deputy Prime Minister Norodom Chakrapong[6] and Interior Ministry senior figures. Prince Sihanouk took the decision to announce the short-lived "National Government of Cambodia" with himself as Head of State, Prime Minister, Supreme Commander of the Armed Forces and Police, and with Hun Sen and Prince Ranariddh as Deputy Prime Ministers. Late on 3 June Prince Ranariddh's written reply expressed "great surprise", and asked a number of questions which effectively put Sihanouk's public assertion that his son had accepted the new government in doubt. The next morning the Palace issued a short statement in which Prince Sihanouk renounced formation of the government, citing Cambodian and U.N. staff objections. He later added that the United States had opposed such an entity. In a 4 June meeting with Sihanouk, Chea Sim maintained that the CPP had made sufficient concessions.

CPP kept the pressure on. The next effort, widely viewed as more of theatre than of reality, was a "secession". Prince Sihanouk told the 10 June meeting of the SNC that Prince Chakrapong and Interior Minister Sin Song had left to establish an "autonomous zone" in Prey Veng, Svay Rieng, and Kompong Cham provinces with others perhaps to follow. A communiqué dated 12 June put the zone under Prince Chakrapong, Sin Song, and Bou Thong, former Defence Minister and electoral victor in Ratanakiri province. It added Stung Treng, Ratanakiri, Mondolkiri, and Kratie to the would-be zone.

Details remain to be elaborated, but the secessionists appear to have used a contingency plan the CPP elaborated when Vietnamese troop withdrawal made creation of a redoubt of the provinces on the east bank of the Mekong seem a good idea. Violence and intimidation threatened provincial non-CPP party offices and members. Demonstrations took place against UNTAC itself, and on 12 June, even Prince Sihanouk joined, or was induced, to urge UNTAC to withdraw from the secession zone.[7] UNTAC publicly rejected the notion.

The role of the Vietnamese is unclear although Hanoi has consistently stated its support for the electoral results and the Paris Agreement. An intriguing, if unconfirmed, item in the *Far Eastern Economic Review* of 1 July 1993 reports that Vietnamese President Le Duc Anh met secretly with Chea Sim "shortly after Cambodia's U.N.-sponsored May election" and told the Cambodian leader that Vietnam would not support a secession, thereby discouraging mass CPP embrace of the notion.

Clearly, the CPP used the event to pressure FUNCINPEC and tried to stampede UNTAC into adding its own pressure to make Prince Ranariddh more conciliatory. A FUNCINPEC statement of the same day scored the CPP for trying to "blackmail" the political process by the secession threat and accompanying violence against FUNCINPEC and UNTAC. While the political leadership was engaging in threatening and divisive gestures, the CPAF itself joined with the two other factional forces and moved a major step forward towards Cambodia's future. A 10 June communiqué of the Cambodian

Armed Forces Chiefs of the General Staff announced commitment of the armed forces to the government that would emerge from the election and identified the armed forces henceforth as "the Cambodian Armed Forces", eventually responsive to the direction of a supreme commander agreed on through the political process.

Movement towards coalition and compromise went forward beginning with Prince Ranariddh's 13 June return to Phnom Penh. UNTAC publicly reminded the SOC of its responsibility to keep order and declared announcements of secession to be "in violation of international law, the territorial integrity of Cambodia and the Paris Peace Accords". The SOC Defence Ministry issued an "Appeal" to officers and combatants of CPAF in the three provinces to maintain order and to negotiate and compromise any "dissatisfaction".[8] The Constituent Assembly opened the next day and gave Prince Sihanouk "full and special powers" as Head of State, formally overturning the deposition of the Prince effected by the National Assembly on 18 March 1970.

Hun Sen travelled to Kompong Cham that afternoon and the secession effectively ended with the reported flight of Prince Chakrapong to Vietnam the next morning. A series of declarations from provincial leaders dated 14 June repudiated or denied secession. Prince Sihanouk himself, in a letter dated 15 June, appealed to "His Royal Highness and Their Excellencies the Leaders of the 'Samdech Euv Autonomous Zone'" to end it. The Prince followed up by receiving Chakrapong, Sin Song, and Hun Sen on 17 June to thank the secessionists for obeying his order. Sihanouk subsequently named Prince Chakrapong to the rank of four-star general for his earlier services and his ultimate responsiveness in ending the secession.

The shape of the compromise became apparent with the midday 16 June broadcast of Prince Sihanouk's proposal for a co-prime ministry shared between FUNCINPEC and the CPP, with himself as head of state of a "Provisional National Government of Cambodia". Sihanouk ultimately agreed to become Supreme Commander after formally proposing the job go to the UNTAC Force Commander. On 18 June, in a large meeting at the Palace for visiting officials of the Permanent Five Members of the Security Council and other interested nations, Prince Ranariddh confirmed acceptance of the concept of parity with the CPP in the provisional authority. In a series of meetings and at entertainments that day and night, Ranariddh, Chea Sim, and Hun Sen agreed on co-prime, defence, and interior ministries. The final division of ministerial portfolios roughly followed Prince Sihanouk's suggestion of 45 per cent FUNCINPEC, 45 per cent CPP, and 10 per cent BLDP as the CPP got twelve ministries and FUNCINPEC eleven; the BLDP leads three and Moulinaka, one. The Constituent Assembly ultimately voted confidence in the provisional administration at its 2 July session.

THE FUTURE

Elements of the short- and medium-term future have emerged. In the shortest term, the vital question is whether the international community will produce the small sums needed to fund the civil service, the military, and the police. This will determine social stability and nurture a process of reforming coalitions of interest. Also in the immediate future, but of impact for at least the next year, will be the creation of the Cambodian Armed Forces, promised in the Chiefs of Staff communiqué of 10 June. The structure and membership of a new, constitutionally based Cambodian government rests on the quality of Prince Ranariddh's leadership; on the intentions of the CPP in removing many important party personalities from the

Constituent Assembly process and, of course, on Prince Sihanouk's own efforts to take a role and the political élite response, especially if the Prince seeks *de facto* executive power or would rely on his prestige. Finally, the future turns on what Khmer Rouge concessions accompany their July 1993 effort to return to the Phnom Penh political process.

FUNCINPEC has compromised on the provisional government, thus realistically recognizing the greater administrative, military, and financial weight of the CPP. The question is whether the provisional formula for sharing can, or should, persist beyond the transitional period. At issue is whether the sides can reform their interests and/or learn to work with each other well enough to be willing to let the new government start with a normal structure. If the new government also uses the clumsy structure of shared key portfolios, including the prime ministry, a real question mark would hang over its capability and credibility, especially in the eyes of the international community. Prince Ranariddh's political skill will be fully tested as part of this process.[9]

CPP moves within the new coalition loom particularly important, as Jakarta Radio noted on 3 July, adding the view that the results embarrassed Hun Sen and put at risk "important trade agreements" with Thai and Malaysians. Jakarta radio saw possible CPP factionalism affecting compromises needed with FUNCINPEC, but voiced a hope for the future with emergence of a moderate faction through such compromise.[10] Many CPP activists resigned seats just before the Constituent Assembly met, to be replaced by party technocrats lower on the candidate lists. Analyses differ on whether the CPP thereby showed its serious intention to use expertise to participate fully in national political life, or whether the CPP was keeping an option open for parallel, even clandestine, party activities to preserve options in the countryside.[11]

The Party of Democratic Kampuchea

Meanwhile, with Khieu Samphan's 13 July 1993 brief return to Phnom Penh, the Party of Democratic Kampuchea (PDK) is poised to resume united front efforts. Having failed to intimidate the electorate, the other parties, and UNTAC into postponing or abandoning the election, the PDK has fallen back onto its own alternative plan.

The overall PDK strategy seeks to conserve forces for the day when the leaders may be able to use them. Their tactic has been to forestall the creation of a legitimate government that would use foreign assistance to build a national armed force that might use the PDK as its target. This fear explains the very violent PDK public rejection of a 6 July agreement between the French and the Provisional National Government of Cambodia for "technical assistance necessary for constituting a national army, in association with States desiring to join in this effort".[12]

The PDK alternative plan is to become part of the political process and obviate becoming a target. Khieu Samphan has put the PDK in favour of participation in the new national armed forces. Even before his 13 July expression of interest, some PDK military field commanders had made a show of willingness to consider easing relations with UNTAC.

On the political front, by 5 July four PDK figures had arrived back in Phnom Penh amid speculation that the next step may be to reanimate the National Unity of Cambodia Party (NUCP) created under Khieu Samphan's presidency on 30 November 1992, and embark on yet another iteration of united front tactics. On 1 July Chan Youran called on Prince Sihanouk and, according to Sihanouk, asked "to become simply a political party".[13] The PDK radio report on its officials' return to Phnom Penh noted that the first two arrivals included Youran, described as a "senior founding member" of the NUCP as well as Mak Ben, also on the founding committee.[14]

Khieu Samphan's 13 June meetings with Prince Sihanouk, with Prince Ranariddh, and with Deputy U.N. Special Representative Behrooz Sedry included his assumption that the PDK is back to stay, and expressed willingness to become "advisers" rather than members of the government as Prince Ranariddh offered, according to Khieu Samphan. Prince Sihanouk declared that the Khmer Rouge personality had offered to join the Cambodian National Armed Forces and become (Permanent) "Counsellors" to the new government. Sihanouk added that Khieu Samphan accepted to return the recently seized monument of Preah Vihear and the Pailin area to the Cambodian state if his proposals were accepted. The Prince concluded by noting his own suggestion of a "Roundtable" of Khieu Samphan meeting of the two of them, Prince Ranariddh, Hun Sen, and Son Sann or Chea Sim who would represent the National Assembly to be held after Sihanouk's own return in mid-September.[15]

Two strategies are at work here. The PDK aim would be to be well-positioned should the new government stall due to politics, incompetence, inactivity, or failure of the foreign donor community to address its genuine needs in a timely manner. Prince Sihanouk seeks to reduce Khmer Rouge violence to the minimum while holding them at some distance, perhaps believing that as Cambodia returns to normal and with prosperity PDK supporters will flow away from them and towards the new national community.

I don't expect everyone here to follow Cambodia anywhere near as intensively as I do, but the NUCP emerged on 30 November last year when it seemed as if the Khmer Rouge might be willing to have an option of participation. Well, they've apparently decided to exercise that option now, and that option is best described as Plan B.

Plan B is to participate in political life, maybe even eventually in the government, in order that the new government not view you as a target. Plan A, which failed, was to collapse the election through intimidation and violence and forestall the creation of a Cambodian government with domestic and international legitimacy. That failed, so we're now on Plan B.

NOTES

The analysis, conclusions, and descriptions here are personal and do not necessarily reflect those of the United Nations.

1. See, for example, Chea Sim's citation of Hun Sen's pithy view of FUNCINPEC when Chea Sim opened a high school on 29 April (Foreign Broadcast Information Service, hereafter FBIS, BK0405101193), and his reference to voters' judging of Hun Sen's statements at a high school inauguration on 26 April (FBIS BK0305111793).
2. UNTAC regulations set forth in Directive No. 93/5 of 6 April 1993 permitted political broadcasting on television, for example, only during one hour a day of UNTAC-sponsored political broadcasting. Any other programming had to be paid for. SOC TV never justified its extensive coverage of Hun Sen's actual campaign activities with receipts.
3. Jacques Bekaert, "Khmer Rouge Could Be at a Turning Point", in the "Cambodian Diary" column, *Bangkok Post*, 5 July 1993, in FBIS BK0507023893.
4. "Incidents of Political Violence, Harassment and Intimidation: 1 March 1993 to 14 May 1993", UNTAC Release.
5. "Safety and Security of the Electoral Process", Statement by Mr Akashi, SNC Meeting, 10 April 1993. In full, the SRSG said, "They [the Phnom Penh authorities] also have an enormous responsibility to put a stop to all further politically-motivated violence. The downward trend in such violence that was apparent during February now seems to have

slowed or reversed, and it is the clear duty of the local authorities to arrest, prosecute or dismiss all officials and others believed to have taken part in election-related violence and intimidation. ... This will call for courage on the part of the leaders of the State of Cambodia Party, who must accept the legitimacy of political opposition."

6. Prince Chakrapong is Prince Ranariddh's younger half-brother. He defected from FUNCINPEC to the SOC in 1991 and in 1992 became a member of the CPP Politburo and Deputy Prime Minister in the SOC.
7. At midday on 12 June Prince Sihanouk, speaking on SOC radio, called for UNTAC to leave the three affected provinces (FBIS BK1206080493 et seq.). At 1800 local time, Radio UNTAC, in Khmer, rebroadcast the Prince's "Message", adding an UNTAC statement that its civilian presence might be reduced to ensure tranquility, but "the military will stay".
8. Signed by Minister Tie Banh (FBIS BK1306150193).
9. Tan Lian Choo made this point trenchantly in her presentation on Cambodia's future.
10. Radio Republik Indonesia, in FBIS BK0307145393.
11. See Nate Thayer, "Surface Calm: Power-Sharing Pact Brings Little Change", *Far Eastern Economic Review*, 8 July 1993, versus Michael Vickery, "Resignation of CPP Candidates and Their Replacements", 24 June 1993 (unpublished paper), which argues for CPP sincerity of intentions. The *Nation* (Bangkok) of 26 June 1993 reports disagreement between Vickery and an UNTAC analyst and academic who take opposing viewpoints on the issue.
12. "Accord entre le Gouvernement de la République Française et le Gouvernement National Provisoire du Cambodge Relatif à la Coopération Technique dans le Domaine de la Défense", signed in Phnom Penh, 6 July 1993 by Co-Prime Ministers Norodom Ranariddh and Hun Sen and Minister of State and Minister of Defence Francois Leotard.
13. Prince Sihanouk's speech after the oath-taking ceremony by the Provisional National Government, 2 July (FBIS BK0307054493).
14. Reporting on the return to Phnom Penh on 1 July on PDK radio is

given in FBIS BK0807051093, which also noted that founding committee members In Sopheap and Kor Bun Heng arrived on 5 July. Announcement of the founding of the party was by Democratic Kampuchea, "Statement by the Founding Committee of the 'National Unity of Cambodia Party', Pailin, 30 November 1992". PDK radio announced on 2 December 1992 the Political Program of the NUCP (FBIS BK0212114592).

15. See "Khmer Rouge Willing to Join New National Army", *Bangkok Post*, 14 July 1993, and "Communiqué de Samdech Preah Norodom Sihanouk du Cambodge, Phnom Penh, le 13 Juillet 1993".

THE CAMBODIAN ELECTION
Whither The Future?

Tan Lian Choo

One of the most notable characteristics of assessing recent events in Cambodia is the fact that time-frame matters considerably whenever you take stock of the situation proper.

The political situation was intractable for a long period of time before the election, as many frustrated Cambodia watchers (such as Tim here!) will testify. However, political manœuvring by the key Cambodian players before, during, and immediately after the election was so intense and such a constant that it frequently triggered changes in their own positions. The Cambodian players were constantly reacting to their own changes in assessment, brought about no doubt by their own perceptions of the manœuvring of their opponents or rivals. But these perceptions could be based on substantial evidence gathered by their own intelligence network, or, in many cases, merely based on personal hunches or even prejudices.

To put it in a nutshell, I would describe the political situation in Cambodia simply as "a situation in which everybody is reacting to everyone, all the time".

That's why political stamina is so crucial for Cambodian players. Of course, Cambodian leader Prince Norodom Sihanouk had, and still has, a lot to do with this. But I will come back to this energetic, complex, and oftentimes impossible figure later in this discussion. For the time being, it is important to note that his return to Phnom Penh, on the eve of the election, did help considerably to alleviate the tense pre-election situation.

Actually, survival is the name of the game for all Cambodian leaders. Ordinary Cambodians know this, especially those in the capital city and provincial towns. So they, too, often suspend judgement of their political leaders until the picture becomes clearer to them. This does not mean they are not reacting — the grapevine is a powerful source of change in Cambodia, and an indispensable part of the Cambodian political system is the rumour mill, which works overtime at moments of crisis or high tension. What it means is that people can think one thing one day, then change their view or belief the next day or even that same night, depending on what they hear has happened in between.

So, when we talk about the situation on the ground — "before" and "during" the election — we have to be quite specific about how long before that we are referring to, and what period of time we are concerned with during the election proper, which lasted six days (23 to 28 May) and of which the results could not be announced till much later.

Let's take one time-frame at a time, starting with the "before" part.

BEFORE THE ELECTION PROPER

Towards the end of April and during the first week of May, the situation on the ground was very, very gloomy for UNTAC and for the then opposition (formerly resistance) parties.

The most significant factor then was — as all of you here must have read from news reports including mine — the fear of armed attacks by the Khmer Rouge to disrupt the election.

Against this (then) potentially violent backdrop, there were, officially, twenty political parties registered for the U.N.-organized polls. This gave the impression that there was a growing political plurality when actually there never was such a development in the first place. Each party needed to have at least 500 registered members before qualifying to stand for election. UNTAC, officially a neutral authority, took great pains to appear as if it took each party seriously — it gathered facts on each party's political rallies, whether it did stage one or some in the first place, and if it did, it recorded the estimated crowd response that it drew.

As the election campaign drew towards its close in the second week of May, it was clear to even the most undiscerning among UNTAC officials that only a handful of the twenty parties were actually capable of making any impression on the Cambodian people. Most of the parties did not even hold rallies, and if one or two of them did, they attracted ridiculously small crowds, of ten or fewer people. One party was even on record as having had one person attend the rally.

Why was this so?

I think by the time the election campaign kicked off (that is, mid-April), the Khmer Rouge threat was so real that would-be Cambodian voters were not about to waste their time with the more

"Mickey Mouse" versions of political representation. Political violence had snowballed; people were well aware of the relentless harassment, intimidation, and in many cases outright assassination campaign waged by the incumbent Cambodian People's Party (CPP). In short, people understood that the CPP was not about to give up power.

The Buddhist Liberal Democratic Party (BLDP), plagued by internal dissent on its strategy, dithered — its leader, Son Sann, wanted out, have no part in the election, while its senior officials wanted to go ahead with what they believed was their one and only fighting chance to win a number of representative seats. In the event, these second-echelon BLDP leaders were proved right, and they now hold a balance of power in the newly elected, 120-seat Constituent Assembly.

FUNCINPEC, a French acronym for the National United Front for an Independent, Peaceful, and Co-operative Cambodia, bore the brunt of the political damage inflicted by the CPP. Prince Norodom Ranariddh, Prince Sihanouk's son, leader of FUNCINPEC, had earlier proved quite popular in towns and in large sections of the countryside. This was also the case in key densely populated provinces like Kompong Cham, widely regarded initially as a CPP stronghold.

But by 1 May, Prince Ranariddh was a discouraged man. He also faced internal calls to withdraw from the polls. Within his party, he sought a collective decision, and insisted that the responsibility involved in this decision to go ahead and participate in the polls be shared among his senior aides, because so many of his people had actually been killed.

The bloody intimidation was very real and everyone around him expected to be targets of annihilation. They often retreated to "safe havens" (usually to homes of different friends in order to keep their movements discreet) as early as 4 p.m. The crowds of FUNCINPEC supporters — ordinary Cambodians who had gathered daily in front of their party offices — had also disappeared. No one dared to stand in front of these premises lest a passing motorcyclist launches a hand grenade (by the way, the crowds reappeared after FUNCINPEC won the election).

So, ordinary Cambodians were very scared during the run-up to the polls. CPP leaders in the mean while "grew in confidence" that they had "swung" possible voter preferences with their intimidation campaign. FUNCINPEC grew restless about not being able to capture the ground that earlier had looked quite sweet.

People saw FUNCINPEC being defeated through the CPP's sheer immoral use of force. It's like when you watch a big bully hit someone and you haven't got the physical strength, mental ruse, or moral courage to do anything about it.

People kept whispering to one another that it may not be wise to vote for FUNCINPEC — this was the pragmatic reaction by ordinary Cambodian survivalists — since a CPP defeat could lead to a worse clash. They feared a FUNCINPEC victory that meant unsettling the CPP's hold on power and possibly triggering an intolerable backlash of violence instigated by the disgruntled losers. At the same time, people were quite fed up with this constant abuse of power. They had been subjected to this kind of abuse for so long; they were having a hard time making ends meet, and they could see the CPP leaders had enriched themselves considerably through corrupt means.

Radio UNTAC, to Tim and his team's credit, launched an aggressive and effective political campaign to promote voter participation, addressing directly this problem of political intimidation and harassment. Radio UNTAC portrayed life-threatening situations in Cambodian homes; assured would-be voters over and over again that their vote would be secret, and that they could go ahead and lie to whoever was intimidating them that they were intending to vote for them when actually they could exercise their free choice once they were in the polling booth alone.

Well, Cambodians responded to this. They felt UNTAC actually understood their predicament *vis-à-vis* their so-called leaders. And at that point, things started to change. People started to whisper around the assurances that UNTAC had given, such as there was no such thing as a secret electronic eye to detect who they were voting for.

DURING POLLING

On polling day itself, 23 May, Cambodians came out in record numbers in what was readily recognized by all international observers as a statement by the Cambodian people that it was casting, collectively, a vote for peace. Some voters had walked as much as 15 kilometres from their villages to polling stations to cast their ballots. Many were illiterate. They could not understand the complicated ballot paper with twenty party symbols. There were quite a number of spoilt votes.

Nevertheless, there was euphoria among UNTAC officials who felt their mission had been a success with total voter participation approaching 90 per cent, a level that had not at all been anticipated because of the violent campaign preceding it. Opposition politicians and voters felt vindicated. FUNCINPEC immediately translated this high voter turn-out to be a pending victory for itself.

Prince Sihanouk was elated, and, as usual, he could not contain himself and had to seize the opportunity at hand to make political capital (even though he had not stood for election).

He declared the voter turn-out was a "historic defeat for the Khmer Rouge", which he said would be wiped out of history. He also declared the Khmer Rouge would be excluded from a future government — he had earlier reiterated that the Khmer Rouge had to be asked to participate in a national reconciliation government. Whenever Sihanouk declares or announces a future scenario, it does not mean that by some magic, it will turn out the way he says it will. He does not lead an administration in the way a chief executive does. But what it does mean is that every party will react to his statement, draw their own conclusions and plot their next moves. So his declarations in fact trigger further manœuvres, or reassessments, on the part of everyone else, including UNTAC chief Yasushi Akashi's. Perhaps Tim can give more colourful details since he is more privy to such developments.

By the end of polling week, CPP leaders were nervous enough to prepare numerous complaints about alleged election irregularities in order to cry foul when the results were officially announced. It also launched a propaganda offensive, accusing Radio UNTAC of being biased since it reported partial results that gave the impression that FUNCINPEC was leading in the counting.

The actions and reactions of the CPP at the time left little doubt that the party was still controlled and led by leaders and cadres who were old-style totalitarian rulers. They had earlier seen the election as an exercise merely to legitimize their rule, and they were truly incapable of conceiving defeat. Since it had never before worked to win a popular election held without coercion, the enormity of the pending defeat left leaders such as Hun Sen almost shell-shocked. For this reason, the post-election secessionist move that was spawned later was quickly recognized by many as a move by Phnom

Penh to secure a bargaining chip for negotiations on the future government. They succeeded in that, by the way.

IMMEDIATE POST-ELECTION PERIOD

When Prince Sihanouk first announced his interim government — one in which he held full executive powers — on the night of Friday, 4 June, he staged what an UNTAC official called a "constitutional coup". He was very much piqued by this criticism and the subsequent international media attention.

In fact, to many of us who had earlier seen him in November 1991 during his historic return to Cambodia after the signing of the Paris peace accords, he was attempting to carry out what he had initially planned and declared but had not succeeded. At that time, he literally forced Ranariddh to join in a political alliance with Hun Sen, announcing that their two parties would merge and that he was embracing Hun Sen as his own "son", just like Ranariddh. Little did Sihanouk know then that Hun Sen alone could not control the CPP.

This time around, Sihanouk was more experienced in his dealings with the CPP. He held talks separately with Hun Sen and Chea Sim, the real power behind the CPP, and also met separately with Phnom Penh armed forces figures who were basically coming forward to offer him their support. So, an electorally defeated CPP was now playing its Sihanouk card. Publicly, the Cambodian leader declared he was acting in the spirit of national reconciliation. Privately, and to the consternation of FUNCINPEC senior activists, he had cut the deal with CPP with little regard for the FUNCINPEC electoral victory or political legitimacy.

So Ranariddh found himself in this dilemma, of having won an election on the strength of his association with his father, but having this very victory robbed by him even before the results were officially endorsed by the United Nations.

What was the reaction on the ground then? People were generally confused, and worried. On the one hand, they really wanted Sihanouk to stay as their leader because they believed he alone had the stature to deal with those who have excessively relied on the use of force; on the other hand, they were disturbed that Sihanouk appeared to be repudiating the election itself by playing along with the CPP in its game since the arrangement was being rejected by FUNCINPEC.

Ranariddh held firm but it also became apparent to his close advisers that they risked losing some of their hard-earned popular support if they continued to cross swords with Sihanouk. So, eventually, there was a softening of positions, and Ranariddh was forced — from the *realpolitik* point of view — to accept the interim coalition government proposal. He knew, just as his father knew all along, that the CPP would not give the planned draft Constitution its support unless its place in government was assured. The draft charter needs a two-thirds majority before it can be accepted by the Constituent Assembly. Ranariddh's only condition for power sharing, in the end, was that the CPP had to recognize the election results first.

So now you have an incredibly cumbersome cabinet of over sixty interim ministers, who are supposed to do some real work but who are not likely to achieve much before end of August, which is when UNTAC pulls out (People like Tim are leaving even earlier!).

WHITHER THE FUTURE?

From all that I said earlier, you can conclude that it's very hard to predict Cambodia's future. There are always many question marks because nothing is as pat as we would like it to be as analysts. So from my own viewpoint, I have mapped out three main inter-related issues at this point, to guide me in my future analysis.

The first is Ranariddh's success or failure as a future modern leader of Cambodia. Can he succeed in bringing about a new generation of Cambodian administrators who are prepared to put aside old scores, pure greediness for money and power, and really have the commitment to rebuild the country to give ordinary Cambodians a decent life? Will the likes of Hun Sen go along with him as a new leader, or are they just waiting to pounce on him? Will his father help him or, on the contrary, undermine his efforts?

All the other countries in Southeast Asia, including here in Singapore, have over the past twenty years nurtured such a generation of new leaders. I believe that Cambodians are also looking forward to something like that but whether or not it comes to pass is a big question mark, of course. Tim has touched on this in his introductory remarks about the political maturity of Cambodian; we never know when it is going to happen. But I do believe — having talked to a number of people and seen a number of them there — that this is something that in fact, deep down in their hearts they want, and this is really their hope. But of course, they haven't got the institutions and the ability to express themselves except for that one time when they could cast their votes.

The next area to watch out for, in my view, is to monitor what happens to CPP stalwarts like Chea Sim. Tim touched on the observation that many of the key party stalwarts have been excluded from the Constitutional Assembly, from the constitutional process and also from the interim government. Will they still call the shots in their party? Will security forces not officially under their charge be prepared to ignore their unofficial orders? Are they planning a sinister underground alternative chain of command? After all, none of them figure in the new interim administration, which has representatives from the CPP side who are more "Western-educated", all of whom were chosen precisely to present an acceptable face of the CPP to the outside world. Could they have given up their claim to power so readily with no *quid pro quo*?

And finally, related to the above questions, is the state of the so-called newly merged armed forces. Will its command leadership be backing the new government, or will it be playing its own games *vis-à-vis* an elected coalition government? Are they interested in staying out of politics or is it greedy for material wealth; is military leadership seen as a means to enrich oneself materially?

These are all worth looking out for, so that if and when there is a *coup d'état*, none of us here will be too shocked.

DISCUSSION

Chairman

Over the last twelve years when ASEAN was working with the Cambodians to bring about the Cambodian settlement, ASEAN diplomats have often described Cambodian political behaviour as doing a *ramwong*, a very intricate dance, a Cambodian dance, very beautiful. It moves slowly, very subtly; some moves are by flickers of fingers, three-way split of the torso, but all that adds up to the Cambodian dance, a beautiful dance. I think our two speakers have described today a very intricate process, the Cambodian *ramwong* in terms of its politics and the election. But they have left, in fact open for the moment, questions about the future, which I think most of you would be very keen to discuss. Our last speaker raised a few points touching on this. I am sure Mr Carney, who is still an official of UNTAC, will find his way of trying to deal with your questions. And now I turn the floor over to you. Can we have the first question, please?

Question

The attention now seems to be focused on the CPP and the FUNCINPEC. What about the Khmer Rouge? Has it been marginalized? Do you see it in any important role in the future? And then the second one, on a more general level, how safe is Cambodia, especially Phnom Penh, for the ordinary visitor?

Tim Carney

The Khmer Rouge. Well, there you've got a little bit of a problem of the formal structure of the Paris Agreement, which remains intact, versus the political realities. Lian Choo made the point which I want to stress as strongly as I can, citing Prince Sihanouk. The Khmer Rouge suffered an enormous defeat as a result of the election. Khieu Samphan, through the entire electoral period was stating on radio, "The Voice of the Great National Union Front of Cambodia", that the election was purely and solely to legitimize Vietnam's control of Cambodia, and as a result, Cambodians would *not* vote. 89.4 per cent of the 4.7 million registered Cambodian voters, themselves 97 per cent of the estimated possible total of eligible Cambodians, went and cast their ballots. This was an incredible rejection of the Party of Democratic Kampuchea. What they are undertaking now, as I have said earlier, is Plan B: to try to wiggle their way, using their continuing legal status as a signatory of the Paris Agreement back into the political structure.

I can speculate a little bit now about Prince Sihanouk's own motives. Prince Sihanouk basically does not want to see the Khmer Rouge forced into isolation to the point that they have to pick up their weapons and fight. He wants to keep violence down. And that's fair enough. At the same time, the actual structure of their participation in the new government may prove in a way that Lian Choo has so masterly described, elusive if not contradictory, if not even unrealizable. In other words, while the country goes forward, the Khmer Rouge may not line up a target of the National Army. But the hopeful economic and social development will attract supporters away from them and marginalize them. Ultimately, they would be just simply dissolved.

Chairman

Before I call on Lian Choo to answer the second question, can I just push this a little, Tim. It has been said and speculated by some who have watched the election, scholars who have watched the election, that they believe the Khmer Rouge in fact persuaded their supporters to give their votes to FUNCINPEC when it became clear that FUNCINPEC was in fact going to win. Was this a reading and does the Khmer Rouge now have a certain standing with FUNCINPEC?

Tim Carney

I'll take the question along with all those statistics that UNTAC has collected to note that we have got food for any number of dissertations out there. We are going to see scholarship advancing by leaps and bounds as a result. If you look at the percentage of the votes, the percentage of people under Khmer Rouge control, and even if you argue, in my view incorrectly, that all, say 10 per cent of Cambodians, under Khmer Rouge control might have voted for FUNCINPEC, you have too small an amount to affect the results in any significant way. Now that's the statistician/political scientist's answer. The historian in me would rather say, yes, in some cases, and journalists reported it, the Khmer Rouge said to their villagers: "OK, OK, you can go vote." Basically they knew they lost, their strategy hadn't succeeded, but they added, "If you have to go vote, vote for FUNCINPEC." That I don't think translates into enough grounds to argue that FUNCINPEC owes the Khmer Rouge, which is I think where you're going. And, in fact, let me cite a Cambodian saying which I think makes the FUNCINPEC–Khmer Rouge equation pretty clear: If you're out in the countryside and it's raining and there's a huge muddy swamp you've got to get across, and there's a water buffalo next to you, you use that water buffalo to cross the muddy place. You use something for temporary advantage, and that in my view is what FUNCINPEC has done with the Khmer Rouge since 1981 or thereabouts.

Chairman

Thank you, Tim. Lian Choo, is Cambodia safe for the ordinary visitor?

Tan Lian Choo

Before I get to the practical aspect of it, can I just add to what Tim has said about the Khmer Rouge. I think that even though the focus is on FUNCINPEC and the CPP as political players in the newly defined political arena of Cambodia, the Khmer Rouge can remain a political force as such because it is after all, whether you like it or not, going to be a pressure group. And I think all the players in Cambodia are fully aware of this. The only difference is that everybody is interested not to have them use their arms, but it does not mean that they will actually disappear. So I think in a politically volatile situation, where you have a lot of disgruntlement, whether it is social or political, or even economic, the potential for a group such as the Khmer Rouge to actually capitalize on mass support is always there. I believe that it is not actually a force that has been marginalized. If you look back to Cambodia's recent history, you find that that's how they grew as a political force to begin with. So I think politicians like Ranariddh are fully aware of this, and that his agenda as a newly elected leader does take into account this sort of reality. So he is trying his very best, as I understand it, to create a new kind of Cambodian leadership, the sort that can at least be aware that it is accountable for its actions; to try and promise to Cambodians that they'll have a better life and to try and deliver this, to try to end corruption. These are all actually, of course, easier said than done because there really is no structure to assist him and he has to basically start from scratch. So, too, for the CPP leadership. For the more politicized among them, politicized in the modern sense, the sense of having to go to an election and win an election, they too, I'm sure, are definitely much more aware now of what they've got to do to perform much better as politicians. And waiting in the wings will be the Khmer Rouge plus other elements to capitalize on this if they flounder.

Coming back to whether it's safe to go to Cambodia or not. I'm asked this question very, very often. The simple answer is that Cambodia is very safe if you don't intend to do anything there. It all depends — as in all such situations where there is very little infrastructure, where there is very little law enforcement, etc. — on what you do when you get there. And if you go to a comfortable hotel, you could just as well be in Singapore or Malaysia, and not feel the difference at all. Because there are Singaporean managers running the Cambodiana Hotel and they make sure that your booking is in order and everything is all right. But if you intend to go to the countryside, it depends on where you want to go, which roads you take. Prudence is of course the name of the game. But again, as I said, it all depends on what you intend to do out there.

Question

I like to begin by congratulating UNTAC in general and Tim Carney in particular for the tremendous success of the Cambodian election. I think before the election was held, the conventional wisdom was that it would fail. Very few outside kept faith, and I'm impressed that those inside UNTAC kept faith. And by doing so, they have created a new political reality in Cambodia.

I have two questions as a consequence of that. The first question, with hindsight now, can we look back and say, that to some extent the success of the election was encouraged by the fact that all the outside major powers, original powers, who had in the past conflicting interests inside Cambodia — these conflicting interests translated into different factions in Cambodia — disappeared in the past year or two, and it was this constellation of unanimity of interests of external powers that encouraged the success of the election. All the regional powers, all the major powers, want the election to succeed: China, United States, Vietnam — every one, you mention it.

The second question, looking ahead, is this: If indeed there is this sort of constellation of interests among all the major powers to see a successful, peaceful solution in Cambodia, what road should the international community follow for the next phase? There are two choices, the first choice is "benign neglect", which is that the international community tell the Cambodians: now, we've done enough for you, you're on your own now, we're cutting off all the arms supplies, you succeed or you fail on your own momentum, whether you're Khmer Rouge, or Hun Sen, or Chea Sim, and so on and so forth. Vietnam drops Hun Sen support, Hun Sen and Chea Sim, Khmer Rouge lose all the external support. Is that the best option for Cambodia? The other possible solution is what I would call "benign intervention", which is that the international community continues to maintain a strong presence in Cambodia, where they will be under the U.N. rubric or some other rubric. But the international community continues to play a forceful role in the transitional period until Cambodia is rebuilt again. Which of these two options would both of you recommend?

Tim Carney

The first question is on the effect of resolution of conflicting big power interests. In a word, I would say positive, but not determining. Let me take us back a little bit to roughly 6 February 1992. It was on that date that the Khmer Rouge had a leadership meeting somewhere in their zone, or possibly just inside Thailand. A document emerged from that meeting, possibly from a defector, possibly from an agent of the Phnom Penh authorities and was given to the press. On my reading of it, and every other Cambodian specialists who looked at it, it was Pol Pot talking to senior leadership circles. He basically explained that "China has gone cold". "Fu", who is the Chinese Ambassador, "has essentially gone cold" on the Khmer Rouge. "That China", I think the metaphor he used, "is like a ship moving up to the quay, it has cut its engines, and it's just drifting in". That's the Khmer Rouge's perception from a contemporary document. I believe it is accurate. No one to my knowledge is contending that the Chinese continue in any way their arms and ammunition shipments or even provided unquestioned diplomatic support to the Party of Democratic Kampuchea. While China abstained, if I'm not mistaken on the U.N. Security Council Resolution, which called for a moratorium on timber exports and sanctions on petroleum supplies to factions not implementing the Paris Agreement, China nevertheless supported the follow-up Security Council Resolution about holding the election and carrying on. This was in direct opposition, confrontation if you will, to the interests of the Khmer

Rouge. So yes, your observation first of all is accurate. There was an end to support by important parties behind the Cambodian factions. But I don't think it was determining, because there was sufficient violence accompanying the Khmer Rouge effort to intimidate the electorate into not voting. This was despite what I understand was some fairly tough talk by Bangkok as well as Beijing. I think we would have to be careful on how we judge the extent of the interests of the former major backers of all these players. That's a little bit vague.

But the second question is in the midst of a much more concrete reply. What does the international community do with the new Cambodia? Well, the first thing one does is one provides enough interim money to be able to pay the salaries of the civil servants, police, and military, and that's something that's under way in New York as we talk. We are not talking about huge amounts of money — $20 million for three months, sticks in my mind, that's definitely something that should happen. It may already have been decided in principle; it hadn't been when I left Phnom Penh.

There are a couple of realities to confront as well. First of all, there will be a continuing U.N. presence. That continuing U.N. presence will be first of all through the specialized agencies, UNICEF, WHO, they are all going to be there. UNDP, for example, will be the major player in effecting the continuing Paris Agreement mandate for the reconstruction of Cambodia. There is an $880 million pledged in Tokyo in June a year ago, which remains to be spent in the country. Whether there will be presence of basically a peace-keeping element, or peace-keeping/diplomatic element is something which can only be determined after Cambodia gets a new constitutional government and asks for it. The Security Council absolutely must approve any sort of continuing peace-keeping presence.

On the bilateral side, we already have an example from 6 July that bilateral relations are going to be very important. The French Foreign Minister and the two co-Prime Ministers who are also co-Defence Ministers signed an agreement which anticipates technical co-operation between France and Cambodia in the fields of defence and security. This is all moving forward as we talk. The relative balance, the question of how you do it, that is something the Cambodians would have to work out and with luck, Prince Ranariddh and his colleagues and the people of like mind in the CPP are going to be able to affect the transformation that will enable Cambodia to benefit from both the U.N. assistance for the future, and the bilateral assistance.

Tan Lian Choo

I'll just add a few sentences to what Tim has said. I think between benign neglect and benign intervention, I guess benign intervention is always the better solution. It's very difficult to intervene and be benign as you know, so obviously this is, even if it is a sort of answer, still fraught with problems because the situation in Cambodia is such that the very countries that are interested in having an influence will go ahead and intervene anyway. But this also means that, as Cambodian history has proved time and time again, these very parties will continue to use the different Cambodian parties, one against the other. And by doing so, it just complicates the situation. So if this is going to be possible at all — I won't call it "control" because you can't — one possible way of being fairly involved without being involved to the point of really preventing a Cambodian leadership from exercising its sovereignty is to have an institution of sorts to allow this to happen. This is my short answer to it, really.

Question

I have a question, again on the more practical level. It's been suggested that the landmines strewn throughout the provinces may represent one of the biggest barriers towards development and future progress for Cambodian people outside of the capital. The question is threefold: has there ever been an estimate on how many landmines had been actually strewn, what is the clearing programme, and what is the estimated time of completion?

Tim Carney

Everyone agrees that the mines are a major national problem and the number of injured as a result of these mines continues to go up everyday. People are hurt by these mines. I have never seen an estimate, I don't think anyone would dare to estimate how many mines there are in Cambodia; orders of magnitude go from hundreds of thousands to millions, I simply couldn't say — it's a lot. Everybody has put mines into Cambodia, from the first Indochinese war until this very day, mines are being put into Cambodia. The big tragedy is that they are continuing to be placed as we talk. The various factions have not yet stopped putting mines in.

What's being done about it, I'll have to reach into my memory a little bit here and I stand to be corrected. There is a joint creation in Cambodia that has as its temporary joint heads, Messrs Akashi and Sihanouk. It's called the Cambodia Mine Action Center; the body is envisaged to make a jump to a purely Cambodian body with foreign and international assistance once UNTAC leaves. It is a primary vehicle for dealing with the mine problem in the future. I regret I can't tell you what its budget currently is, or even where it's got its money from to date. I know there have been separate mine-clearing programmes. The Americans, for example (I call them that when I'm in my U.N. role), have given as part of their road-building exercises in the northwest of Cambodia, a fair sum of money for their contractors to clear the roads of mines.

The initial effort has to be to clear your lines of communication, your roads, and then you've got to clear the fields as you get the refugees initially, but to the population in general, to move back on to land — that would have been impossible because it was strewn so heavily with mines before. There are a number of other nations that are interested in mine-clearing. There are a number of private organizations such as the Halo Trust, which have been hired as part of the efforts to clear mines, and as I said, I don't have the statistics with me on the number of hectares that have been cleared, but it's fairly small considering the size of Cambodia.

Question

I would like to pursue the question on external power interest a bit further. We know that countries such as China, Vietnam have put in a lot of investment in this whole conflict, arms and support, and so on. And the reasons for this investment were related to very basic strategic requirements of perception. Are you persuaded that these powers are now prepared to let the situation drift out of their control or, if you would prefer, out of their steer of influence? If they are not, what are the present leverages of influence that they can exercise in Cambodia?

Tan Lian Choo

Actually, I think it's not as simple as that. It's obvious that a country such as France has an interest in wanting to be influential. It's very clear that France has interest in Cambodia for historical, political, diplomatic reasons, etc., and some of us may question the wisdom of their approach, but in all these cases — and Thailand is another one — all these countries have their interests which are in no way mysterious to the rest of the world. So the Cambodians themselves are aware of this. As Tim pointed out earlier, they are actually very sophisticated politically, but it's not a straight line in Cambodia; you can't find a simple tactic or diplomatic strategy or even a political way of doing things and expect that you can have leverage just like that. It is always very difficult to describe what happens in Cambodia.

To many people who are familiar with the sort of manœuvring there, as Heng Chee was saying, it can be like what very often ASEAN diplomats used to say — a kind of a elaborate *ramwong*, that goes around in circles, all kinds of movements that may or may not mean anything. But sometimes I see it as — to illustrate Tim's assessment that they are politically sophisticated — a Chinese checkerboard of sorts, the political game, I mean. You have six parties, all starting at the same time. And there is a very simple rule, you can only jump once, or in a series of one-jump moves. The rule of the game is quite simple. At the same time, when all the seeds get to the centre of the board and nobody can move anywhere, it's quite intractable, and somebody, somewhere has to make a concession that may or may not be an advantage to the other parties. Very often, this just has to be done, otherwise nobody can get out of this situation. And at that point, things may start to sort of move, and if not, if everybody just holds still, doesn't take his turn, nothing happens.

So I think to some extent, it's the same for those powers that want to have an influence. They may want to do something but at different points in time the effectiveness of these actions will vary.

Tim Carney

I see two sets of interests here. One is basically geo-political major power and all of the arguments about the Cold War having ended affecting those interests are obvious so I won't go into them. Rather more interesting are historical leftovers and regional perceptions of interests. I think the interests have certainly changed.

Let me try to illustrate a possible direction of change which also will bear on the future. Thailand and Vietnam have for centuries regarded Cambodia as a buffer between them. Vietnam itself saw Cambodia as an area into which it could easily expand as a culture that was both trivial and in decline if you look at the efforts of the middle of the last century to call Phnom Penh "Nam Vang", to get Cambodians to wear Vietnamese court dress, and speak Vietnamese, and dress their hair. That way you see a little historical aspect that goes along with, in fact tries to reinforce, the geo-strategic aspect of a Cambodia as not only a buffer, but one that might some day be absorbed into Vietnam. Whereas the Thais had feared the ancient possibility of a hostile army poised at the Watthana Gap, which is basically where the towns of Poipet and Aranyaprathet are. That is flat land and as suitable for armour in this day and age, as it was for calvary in the eleventh century, tenth century on up to the invention of the internal combustion engine. What you are seeing now though, on the part of both Vietnam and Thailand — I submit and I put this forward as a suggestion, as a speculation — is a change in the definition of interest, a change in the perception of how you deal with the neighbouring states. One of my Thai friends calls Cambodia "no buffer and it is no buffet either, we're not trying to devour Cambodia". In other words, the Thais see themselves as more confident as their polity internally is sufficiently strong and their external economic capabilities sufficiently developed so that Thailand can deal with Vietnam as another regional player.

Question

How does the presence of the foreigners in UNTAC affect the Cambodians?

Tan Lian Choo

It's very jarring physically when you see foreigners running your country, it doesn't matter who they are, these foreigners. Of course, these foreigners can be wearing blue berets and they drive white cars, but they are foreign. It doesn't mean that they are not liked. To a large extent, UNTAC is very much liked by the Cambodian people, but it's still always jarring for those who are in some ways disgruntled.

If you have been able, as a businessman, to make money out of UNTAC's presence, then as a Cambodian businessman, you would be very happy that UNTAC is there. But if you've been one of these poor Cambodians, who only saw the cost of living going up and so on, then of course, there is reason to believe that this is a very unhappy state of affairs created by the U.N. presence. I think to some extent, people are conscious about it. But if they are not taking UNTAC to task, it's because they know that UNTAC was going to leave anyway. There was a calendar; there was a clear statement that UNTAC would not be there forever. There was in the beginning, in my view, a general dissatisfaction that life had been made much more expensive with the U.N. presence. As the day of reckoning approaches — UNTAC is going to leave — people are beginning to, in a way, also get worried. Although the cost of living has gone up, they are asking themselves, "What are we going to do if our Cambodian leaders who had been fighting all this time, decide to start fighting again?" So, I think, as UNTAC forces approaches the point of being finally withdrawn, people are starting to have other fears. That sort of insecurity is very deep in the Cambodian psyche. I think it's beginning to surface again. So at this point, most Cambodians (I don't mean those who have made some money, because they are obviously getting ready to leave the country, or are already outside, maybe) who have no means of escaping are actually more concerned about the fact that their own security may not be as guaranteed as before. So again, it's a question of when you pose this question. Today, as the withdrawal date gets closer and closer, people are again starting to worry about what's going to happen when UNTAC's gone. You must always remember that the disarmament phase of the whole peace process failed.

With regard to how dangerous Cambodia is, at least eight or nine out of ten people that you meet on the street are armed, or have access to arms. They have means to fire power, one way or another. This is what makes it dangerous, of course. The Cambodians you meet on the street is not going to open fire at you right away. But, well, the fact that such a person is armed, and that large sections of the country remain armed, is a very worrying thing for Cambodians.

Tim Carney

I think Lian Choo has pretty convincingly set forth the Cambodian dimension of the answer. I'll suggest that the effects of a mission the size of UNTAC, 22,000 people, 16,000 battalion members from thirty-two countries, roughly 3,500 civilian police from roughly the same number of countries, and the rest some 2,000 random and not so random civilians — that's a tremendous impact on a country the size of Cambodia with the extensive devastation to its infrastructure. This is a lesson we have to study and look at for future U.N. operations. The operation in Mozambique, for example, is getting under way now.

The world community needs to look and see if there isn't an easier way to have your large presence mediated. Do you put everybody in a camp and let people out with passes to try to keep prostitution down, for example? And to keep rents down, rather than throw maybe 2,000 civilians into the Phnom Penh housing market? The questions are all there, and I sure don't have the answers, but they are nevertheless real.

Question

I would like to first congratulate Tim and his colleagues at UNTAC for what I do not regard as benign occupation but a very important role that the United Nations plays in the rebirth of Cambodia. And I think I should also congratulate Lian Choo for her brilliant reporting. I've a two-part question. The first part is a sequel to an earlier question. And what I like to ask Tim is whether there is any evidence that would enable us to infer that just as China has distanced herself from the Khmer Rouge, Vietnam has also distanced herself from Chea Sim and Hun Sen and the CPP. Can we, for example, construe the failure of Vietnam to support the attempt by Norodom Chakrapong to lead the seven provinces of the east in the secessionist move as such evidence? My second question is to all our panellists, and this is, what is the best role that the ASEAN countries can play in the rebirth Cambodia?

Discussion

Tim Carney

The first question is very carefully formulated. You're looking for evidence to infer that Hanoi has distanced itself from the CPP. Well, that item in the *Far Eastern Economic Review* smacks of it if I may reach into my past as a diplomat. It smacks of a calculated, deliberate, purposeful leak by a senior official of the government concerned. Essentially, somebody wanted it known. Somebody in Hanoi at the most senior level wanted it known that Vietnam was not playing that game. I think that's pretty good evidence.

As I look at other evidences, I think we can cite the very straightforward and rapid public Vietnamese position accepting the election and its results. And that came out very, very quickly and it was absolutely uncategorical. No question of Vietnam's withholding its acceptance of the results of the election. Those two are among the strongest recent evidences I see.

But, I suspect what you're looking for is something that might be a little more, a little harder from perhaps within the diplomatic community or even from discussions with Vietnamese officials. I don't have anything like that myself. But I don't have anything that would cause me to put into question my working assumption based on the evidence cited that indeed Vietnam is prepared to let Cambodian politics unfold. You can be sure that like all of Cambodia's neighbours, Hanoi will want to keep its finger on the pulse, that there will be a very active effort to do that.

There is an enormous question hanging over the relationship between Cambodia and Vietnam concerning the Vietnamese who fled in the wake of Khmer Rouge terror. And there are perhaps as many as a few thousand such people waiting now at the border to go back to Cambodia. I'm talking about ethnic Vietnamese whose families made Cambodia their home for one or two generations. This is a separate problem from the general immigration questions. With that you are talking effectively about refugees. There is another issue that has not been addressed, and it is something that Hanoi would do well to note, concerning the territorial frontier with Cambodia. Parts of that frontier have been shifted, there is no doubt about that at all. And that frontier is fairly well delineated in documents, if I'm not mistaken, and I believe it's the 1954 French maps that the Cambodian factions have taken as definitive. There exists certainly enough modern electronic hardware — you could probably wander out of this hotel and buy one at an adjacent store that gives your latitude and longitude to the nearest 10 metres, just by pushing a button. This is something that ought to be resolved very quickly.

ASEAN has already done a lot. As I started by paying tribute to Singapore's diplomacy at the United Nations and then as the Jakarta informal process got under way, so I can note that all of ASEAN now has a role, or should have a role in Cambodia. How will ASEAN integrate Cambodia into the region? Prince Sihanouk's remarks on the subject have been ambiguous or even put Cambodian participation in doubt, if I recall. Malaysia, as far as I know, is the only ASEAN state with capital investment in Cambodia at this point, although Singapore may have some in the ports at Kampong Som. Thailand, naturally its interests goes without saying, but at the same time, as for Vietnam, Thailand has to be very upfront, showing evidence that it, too, is willing to leave the people it has supported, most notably, the Khmer Rouge themselves to become participants without reservation, mental reservation, in the political process in Cambodia. Indonesia has made a major contribution through the two battalions that have been there. I see ASEAN as a natural future for all of Indochina, in fact.

Discussion

Tan Lian Choo

I don't really have very much to add but just to elaborate a little some of my thoughts about what ASEAN can play. I don't really have simple answers and I don't think anybody has them. It's just that obviously it would be in Cambodia's interest to recognize that its future lies with its own integration with mainstream Southeast Asia. But having said that, it's not so simple for the Cambodians to recognize this either. They have been rather engrossed in their own problems and very often don't really see beyond what the immediate is going to bring them. So right now, as far as the Cambodian players are concerned, they are talking about their own survival as individual political leaders and are more than happy to have any party from outside willing to support them. But, at the same time, this support can be contradictory and they can actually act against each of these players. So to come back to just a few specific countries: Thailand, Malaysia, within ASEAN — they each have their own agenda in a country such as Cambodia. Normally, within ASEAN there is a general understanding that you don't go around criticizing the other ASEAN member for what it is doing in another ASEAN country or another Southeast Asian country. But I believe that in the next decade or so, this should not apply in the case of Cambodia simply because there has been so much diplomatic investment in the situation in Cambodia. Even if a particular ASEAN country does not have an interest to pursue, it does the regional grouping no good to allow the situation to maybe disintegrate to a point where you have one particular ASEAN member having an out and out policy that is objectionable to the rest of the world. So, in a way, the role that the regional grouping such as ASEAN can play, in my view, is actually almost a moral one because you want to have a consensus on what's accepted behaviour and what's not accepted behaviour, basically. If we're going to put our money down in the reconstruction, you would like to see that this money goes a long way, and when there is reconstruction of infrastructure, etc., you don't really want a situation where corruption is so rife that it'll benefit only a few pockets within Cambodia. It doesn't help a country such as Cambodia actually move along and be able to take its place in modern Southeast Asia one day.

Question

I take it's a fact that we all recognize that the United Nations has itself scored a stunning success in providing a service to produce a legitimate election and I take it that Mr Carney has played an important role, which I don't think he's trying to discuss, being part of making the presence of a credibility of this effort a reality for the Cambodians. But I would like to go back to that fact now. Here is a service that the United Nations has provided, it might be available, presumably available to others. Thinking perhaps, as a businessman might, just figuratively, here's a service, I would like to ask both speakers, if they care to speculate about two things. One, what other countries or factions, groups within countries, might want to avail themselves of this service, that is, for their own elections. And secondly, what countries, larger powers perhaps, who would like to get out from under the support of smaller countries, might urge the use of the United Nations to reduce their own commitments and leave behind some semblance of a legitimate government. And just in the interest of speculation, I suggest any place in the world, but if you prefer, Asia.

Tim Carney

I would be lying if I didn't say that such topics figure in occasional discussions particularly among my U.N. colleagues who are on the permanent staff of the Secretariat. There are two aspects about Cambodia which may not be unique but seem to me to be necessary conditions. One is there was an acceptance that the factions had fought to such a point that they recognized the need for an agreement. That may not be unique, but is very important. And the second is that Cambodia was, and in fact still is, basically flattened. There isn't very much depth of political leadership at the moment or there isn't much texture in the fabric called the society. That gives a certain amount of scope for an international effort to come in and succeed as well. Let me illustrate the second point with a contrast — look at South Africa, which some had argued as a potential place for such a U.N. operation. Having served there, I would contend that there is such a depth of South African educated opinion, talented work-force, and rational thinking that that condition is fulfilled by what exists in the country. An agreement seems to be worked out to effect 27 April as a date for a national election. So I'm not sure, for example, that South Africa would require the overwhelming mandate of UNTAC to have many foreigners come into their country in order to run elections. You've got to be in very, very bad shape indeed to let that happen. That was the case with Cambodia. That maybe doesn't answer the question entirely, but it might get some discussion going.

Tan Lian Choo

I think Tim is right to say that things have to be really bad for you to want to have foreigners come and organize things for you. But I think in some ways, the Cambodian case was also different in that the very players themselves could not trust one another, so much so that they thought they could just push this responsibility to outsiders and at the same time take advantage of these outsiders with their presence. So it's actually very complex, the way it all came together, it's just too complex in my view, to actually be reproduced in another situation, whether in Asia or elsewhere.

Having said that, I would like to also say again, what Tim had earlier on said, that it is obviously not very sensible to come into a situation where you have such poor lack of infrastructure and to bring in so many foreigners who are used to a standard of living that is just inconceivable for that society. So overnight, you will create, whether you like it or not, a great social turmoil of sorts, social and economic; the French would say a *bouleversement*. It's just something that you can't control: it has its own dynamics. That, in my view, is a lesson to be learnt from the UNTAC experience in Cambodia. All the officials or diplomats or even the Cambodian players themselves, fought so hard over the Paris Agreement, arguing about the prepositions, and the dots and the crosses and so on, but nobody at that time actually thought in terms of, well, you have to actually bring in the tables and chairs from New York, try and construct offices the way the United Nations works. I think in a way that is the great set-back of the United Nations as a peace-keeping mission because it's so used to working according to all these standard facilities that are available in New York, or in U.N. headquarters. Whether you go to a U.N. office in Paris, or New York, or Geneva or even in Bangkok, in ESCAP, the toilets look the same, the way the offices are built, the materials are the same, and that in itself creates a tremendous logistical pressure on the mission itself in my view. Tim probably has other ideas but he's not a U.N. professional. I think those who come with the United Nations do come with a lot of baggage and that is probably the main problem in the U.N. mission, as such, wherever it may be. Of course, if you put the socio-economic backdrop to this whole thing, then you will see why it's bound to create that sort of disruption.

Discussion

Chairman

Thank you, Lian Choo. I think for the countries that wish to adopt the same formula for elections or for big powers trying to relinquish or find a face-saving way to relinquish their hold on small countries, or other countries, perhaps it's not just whether they would like it. For the United Nations to take on more actions to be a policeman, to play baby-sitter or nanny or whatever, it requires money. I think we all know how expensive the UNTAC operation is, how expensive peace-keeping is, so in the end the United Nations would be affected by this very major critical question before it takes on all kinds of exercises. That's a deciding factor, I suspect.

Well, I think we've come to the end of a very interesting forum. When we decided to hold this forum, to plan this forum initially, I wondered whether in Singapore or elsewhere we have come to a time of Cambodia fatigue. Seeing the audience here today, I'm convinced that in fact, there is continuing interest in Cambodia, because Cambodia is a story, a very tragic story in Southeast Asia in the last couple of decades. And I think most Southeast Asian, ASEAN people, would be interested to see what peace will bring to Cambodia and whether they have a role to play in Cambodia in the future in its reconstruction, and in trying to help develop its people.

I would like to thank our two speakers today, Tim and Lian Choo, for coming from Phnom Penh via Bangkok to be with us and to give us these two very interesting and stimulating presentations and for trying to answer your questions as frankly and as far as they possibly can.

Many I ask you now to join me in thanking them in the usual manner. And I thank you for being such a wonderful audience.

THE AUTHORS

Timothy Carney is Director of the Division of Information and Education, United Nations Transitional Authority in Cambodia.

Tan Lian Choo is a Bangkok correspondent of the *Straits Times*.

ABOUT THE SERIES

Since 1975, Virginia Commonwealth University has sponsored publication, under the general editorship of Walton Beacham, of the winning manuscript in the annual AWP Award Series in Poetry, an open competition for book-length manuscripts. Established in 1974 in a cooperative arrangement between VCU and the University Press of Virginia, the award carries a $500 honorarium and an invitation for the winning author to read at the AWP Annual Meeting.

Manuscripts are received by the series director, who divides them among readers, who are published poets. Finalists are selected and the manuscripts are submitted to a final judge who chooses the winning book. Final judges for the series have included Richard Eberhart, Elizabeth Bishop, Robert Penn Warren, and Donald Justice. Maxine Kumin chose *The Hours of Morning* as the first-place selection in the 1980 AWP Award Series.

For further information and guidelines for submission write: The Associated Writing Programs, Old Dominion University, Norfolk, Virginia 23508.

THE VIRGINIA COMMONWEALTH UNIVERSITY SERIES
FOR CONTEMPORARY POETRY   WALTON BEACHAM, GENERAL EDITOR

Moving Out
    by David Walker   1976

The Ventriloquist
    by Robert Huff   1977

Rites of Strangers
    by Phyllis Janowitz   1978

James Cook in Search of Terra Incognita
    by Jeanne Larsen   1979

Following Gravity
    by James Applewhite   1980

LIBRARY OF DAVIDSON COLLEGE

Books on regular ... for two weeks. Book
must be presented

A fine is charg